Yellow Umbrella Books are published by Red Brick Learning
7825 Telegraph Road, Bloomington, Minnesota 55438
http://www.redbricklearning.com

Library of Congress Cataloging-in-Publication Data
Jiménez, Vita.
[What kind of sound? Spanish]
¿Qué sonidos hay?/por Vita Jiménez.
p. cm.
Summary: "Simple text and photos present different sounds"—Provided by publisher.
Includes index.
ISBN-13: 978-0-7368-5991-2 (hardcover)
ISBN-10: 0-7368-5991-8 (hardcover)
ISBN 0-7368-3089-8 (softcover)
[For CIP information, please refer to http:www.loc.gov]

Written by Vita Jiménez
Developed by Raindrop Publishing

Editorial Director: Mary Lindeen
Editor: Jennifer VanVoorst
Photo Researcher: Wanda Winch
Adapted Translations: Gloria Ramos
Spanish Language Consultants: Jesús Cervantes, Anita Constantino
Conversion Assistants: Jenny Marks, Laura Manthe

Copyright © 2006 Red Brick Learning. All rights reserved.
No part of this book may be reproduced without written permission from the publisher. The publisher takes no responsibility for the use of any of the materials or methods described in this book, nor for the products thereof.
Printed in the United States of America.

Photo Credits
Cover: Carol Werner/Index Stock; Title Page: Skjold Photographs; Page 4: Darel Crawford/Durango & Silverton Narrow Gauge Railroad; Page 6: Gary Sundermeyer/Capstone Press; Page 8: C. Sherburne/PhotoLink/PhotoDisc; Page 10: Stockbyte; Page 12: Ralf Schmode; Page 14: Joe Valbuena/USDA; Page 16: BananaStock, Ltd.

1 2 3 4 5 6 11 10 09 08 07 06

¿Qué sonidos hay?

by Vita Jiménez

Un sonido puede ser fuerte.

Un sonido puede ser suave.

Un sonido puede ser fuerte.

Un sonido puede ser suave.

Un sonido puede ser fuerte.

Un sonido puede ser suave.

¿Qué sonidos haces tú?

Índice

fuerte, 5, 9, 13
haces, 17
puede, 5, 7, 9, 11, 13, 15
ser, 5, 7, 9, 11, 13, 15
sonido, 5, 7, 9, 11, 13, 15, 17
suave, 7, 11, 15